THE LEGACY OF OUR BACKINGS

THE
LEGACY
OF OUR
BACKINGS

*Childhood Memories of Mexborough
in the 60s*

Michael John Fowler

Wharncliffe Publishing Limited

First published in 1995 by
Wharncliffe Publishing Limited

Copyright © Michael John Fowler 1995

*For up-to-date information on other titles produced under the
Wharncliffe imprint, please telephone or write to:*

> **Wharncliffe Publishing Limited**
> **FREEPOST**
> **47 Church Street**
> **Barnsley**
> **South Yorkshire S70 2BR**
> **Telephone (24 hours): 01226-734555**

ISBN: 1-871647-25-8

A CIP catalogue record of this book is available from the British
Library.

Printed in Great Britain by Redwood Books, Trowbridge,
Wiltshire

CONTENTS

This series of nostalgic accounts of my childhood is dedicated with love to Christopher and Kyle, who hopefully will never know the meaning of hard times.

'Everything we are and everything we do, we are part of history'

INTRODUCTION

Listen to historians and they will say that the 1960's was the dawning of a new era. It brought 'flower power' and hippies, a freedom of speech and a breed of youth that stirred a certain angst amongst onlookers.

Work was plentiful yet rewards were poor. Washday blues were supposed to disappear overnight as the housewife swapped her dollytub and scrubbing board for an electrical twin-tub.

In reality this new era merely hid the harshness and poverty that still pervaded the streets and back alleys of the old Victorian housing stock. Accommodation still lacked the basic amenities of a hot water supply, a fixed bath and an inside flush toilet.

It was against this background that I grew and developed.

This series of nostalgic accounts is intended to give a memorable insight into those times. It may seem to some that those days were fun filled and excitingly happy with endless scope for exploring one's roots.

Yet as a child is not all life viewed through 'rose tinted glasses'?

Michael John Fowler

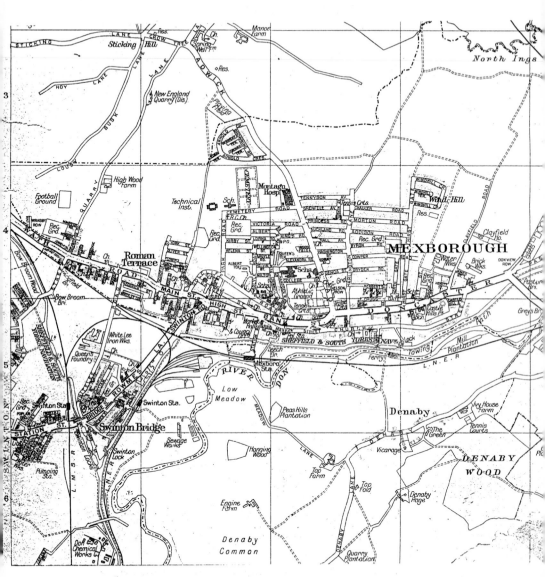

Above: A map of Mexborough showing the street layout during the sixties before the planners got to work.

EARLY YEARS

An upsurge of guerrilla activity in the 1950's, thousands of miles South East of Mexborough became known as the Malaya campaign. It sent an influx of British servicemen, many of them parted from their dear ones for the first time to serve two years National Service in a country which most of them hardly knew existed.

John Kerr Fowler, nicknamed 'Jock' because of a hint of a Scottish accent from his early upbringing, was a skinny 19 year old Yorkshireman.

He left English shores to do his stint with the Air Despatch Corps.

Friendships in those long wooden dormitories came and went but some memories and friends remained forever. One of John's friends was a young conscript by the name of Gordon King, who came from a large but friendly family living in the east end of London.

Letters were not a thing that John regularly indulged in mainly because his family were not exactly close. However, with a little encouragement from Gordon, he began a friendly correspondence with Gordon's dark haired twin sister Dulcie. An invitation to their home in our capital city was pounced upon and a relationship blossomed as John attached himself — and was duly accepted — to the bosom of the King family.

With his service completed in 1956, John returned to Scotland and then moved down to his parents' home situated at 2 Wood Street, Mexborough where he resumed his apprenticeship as a plasterer.

His love for Dulcie flourished during that year and they tied the knot on the 22nd December at the register office in Doncaster.

The early months saw Dulcie uprooted from her family and introduced to her husband's as they rented one bedroom and shared other rooms at Wood Street. The arrangement

Above: Dulcie King married John Kerr Fowler on the 22 December, 1956, at Doncaster registry office.

Above: The rear of 2 Wood Street. This side of the street was demolished in the 1980's and is now a housing complex for aged persons.

Below: The wooden building of Downings second-hand furniture shop was situated on Main Street at the junction with Schofield Street, and was where my parents bought much of their furniture during their early years. This building, together with the two houses to the left hand side, was demolished and made way for Lees D.I.Y. shop.

was at its best strained and at its worst uncomfortable and with the imminent arrival of a baby they negotiated a new start at premises which were part of a shop on Main Street, Mexborough. It was a mere stone's throw from Wood Street. In fact an alleyway on Wood Street ran to the shared courtyard of their new home.

Almost nine months from the date of their marriage a bouncing, lively, blue eyed boy arrived on 25 September, 1957. I was christened Michael John.

The enclosed yard of Main Street brought relative safety in those days and it was there I met my first friend Tony Sharp. In the early days there was lots to investigate in this enclosure. There were a myriad of outside toilets and a large wash house, with whitewashed walls, two stone sinks and

Above: The rear courtyard between Main Street and Wood Street. The house in the background belonged to the Sharp family and my first friend, Tony, lived there.

several metal dolly tubs and scrubbing boards.

In a far corner of that yard was old Mrs Squires' house. Mrs Squires was a small, wiry and sometimes fearsome lady, who chided us regularly if we dared to play near her kitchen door. However, on her good days I was invited in to taste her home made buns and biscuits that she cooked in the oven of her large black fire range. Her house seemed immaculate, with everything polished and gleaming, particularly the black range. Trailing house plants hung everywhere. My recollection of this small petite lady is a face with skin the colour and texture of parchment, framed by snowy white hair tied neatly into a bun. She always wore sombre black. In the early morning I would regularly spy her donkey-stoning her step. On those occasions when she invited me inside her home, I would negotiate that white line with some trepidation.

We only stayed in that house, at the back of the shop, for just over a year because two heart stopping incidents changed our circumstances. The first was during the early months of Mum's second pregnancy — later to deliver my sister Glynis — when she received an electric shock from the old and decrepit socket in the kitchen. The second incident was when hot ashes fell out of the ancient fire, badly in need of repair, setting fire to the room carpet and sending panic and fear rushing through the very minds of my parents. This spurred them to negotiate a mortgage for the princely sum of £600 to purchase a three bedroom terraced house at 23 Schofield Street, Mexborough. In July 1960 2 months before my third birthday we moved house and this was where my grounding for future life began.

HOME SWEET HOME /
THE BETTERWARE MAN

Upon reflection, during the autumn and winter months there was something nostalgic, almost quaint, about the cheery coal fire that burned in the grate of the large mottled green range in the middle room — the living room, — of the three bedroom terraced house. Move out of that room and your breath took on a life of its own, a wisp of fog appeared between clenched teeth, as the sudden chill within the other rooms enveloped you and clung on until you leapt back into the warmth again.

The grip of winter that pervaded everything outside, covered glass panes in delicately traced ice patterns. Cold draughts crept between gaps in the sash windows. It was on these occasions that one of the small Victorian fireplaces situated in two of the bedrooms was lit. It spluttered into life as a dull, smoky fire, with Mother holding a section of newspaper over the front of the grate, endeavouring to rouse it into more cheerful action. I would sit deep in thought, chin resting on hands, gazing at the newsprint. I knew that if it took an unexpected and sudden hold a brown scorch mark would appear, throwing Mum into a panic. Her hands would beat the paper in a frenzy and she would curse between clenched teeth.

As the fire burnt, I watched the leaping and dancing flames. Then a sudden back-draught would catch me unaware, sending a plume of black smoke back into the room and forcing me to retreat into a corner, coughing and choking on the thick belching clouds.

During those cold winter months I would lay in bed and blow out great gulps of air and watch the steam like vapour rise until it disappeared. The beds, with extra piles of itchy grey blankets, were warmed with bricks that had been heated in the oven of the fire range and then wrapped in an old towel. The heat from these lasted longer than any hot water bottle. The only drawback was when a corner became exposed. The burning sensation was instantaneous and my legs would whip upwards towards my stomach, finger-tips rubbing at the burnt toe and examining it in the dark for blisters.

On a rimy night, when an early hoar frost was covering everything, going to the toilet was the last thing a young boy needed. Add to this a cloudy sky and an impenetrable darkness where each shadow hid a malevolent entity, and my speed towards the brick outhouse and toilet increased

Below: The outside 'loo' at the bottom of the yard was the night time sanctuary for all manner of outdoor evils that a child's imagination could conjure up.

dramatically. The gap beneath the door threw out a flickering yellow glow from the 'tilly' lamp that clung to a lagged water cistern. In the short time I sat on the toilet my little foot would be stretched to its limit forcing shut the door, which had become a shield against an unknown foe that I imagined lurked outside. My eyes focused on a spider that hung from a wet and clammy web, suddenly visible. My ears strained for any strange noises. The dash back to the safety of the kitchen door broke any hundred yards sprint record.

The cellar was a dark place, a stone-walled pit in the depths of the house, that would flood from seeping water as the rain fell into the road above. In my early years, to keep me away from this place, I was told that a creature called Jabus dwelt there. This mythical creature was some kind of devil's helper who just loved naughty boys. Jabus

Below: The tin bath was 'housed' in the basement of the cellar and dragged up mainly on a Sunday evening by mi dad who seemed to be not the least bit scared of the mysterious Jabus.

became a thing to fear. As I grew older and was given the chore of bringing up the coal, my arms would shovel like pistons, ferreting in the dark to fill the bucket, with my eyes staring into the blackened corners. I was convinced on more than one occasion that a pair of eyes blinked back at me.

As the winter took its grip, Dad was occasionally laid off work, unable to mix plaster because of the frozen water. At such times the household budget was squeezed tight. I remember my sister and I learning to make briquettes from a combination of coal-dust and a weak mixture of cement that was forged into an oblong block. The resulting coal brick burned and crackled incessantly, sometimes spitting out red hot shards that would force me back from the peggy rug and into the confines of the sofa, until the fire had died down.

Originally there was no bathroom in the house and so Mum would wash me whilst I stood on the metal draining board at the side of the pot sink. The only hot water 'on tap' came from an electrically heated water boiler called a 'geyser' that was fixed to the kitchen wall. Sunday night was bath night. Endless pans of water, boiled on the fire range and cooker, were emptied into a tin bath brought up from the cellar to be placed in front of the fire. Memories of winter nights with the room light off and the fire embers glowing, keeping one side of the bath warm, filter back as though it was yesterday.

'You're peeping' said Glynis.

'I'm not.' I insisted, closing the gap in my fingers to blur out my sister's shape.

'You were and you know it.' she snapped back.

'All right I'll count again.' As I began my numbers I heard the patter of my sister's feet ebbing away into the room. Hide and seek was one of our favourite games. There were so many nooks and crannies to venture into, and even the cellar was braved as we grew older.

I can recall that one day whilst playing with cousin Sue,

who was the finder, I made a suggestion to Glynis as to where she could hide. I had decided to hide in the outhouse behind the large builder's wheelbarrow, but Glynis was looking for a new place. I decided to help her. In our yard was an old battered metal dustbin which had just been emptied and it seemed the ideal place. I had never actually seen the lid fit correctly, but I found that with a little pressure it clipped down perfectly. The minutes ticked by and I was soon found, but Sue could not find Glynis and eventually gave up.

It was now I realized why I had never seen the lid fit correctly — it was stuck fast! No matter how hard we tugged at it the lid would not budge. Glynis's screams grew louder and louder until they attracted my Mum. She appeared from the kitchen door rubbing her hands on a tea towel. As soon as she realized what had happened, hearing the muffled cries from within the bin, she bellowed at me. Even she had difficulty in prising off the lid and when she eventually did Glynis emerged looking like a golliwog. Hard as I tried I could not help but giggle at the sight of Glynis scrambling from her metal cage wide-eyed with a mixture of fear and relief. Her blackened face was streaked with tears.

My giggling stopped when I felt the slap of my mother's hand around my ear.

The ringing in my ears faded as a familiar sound got louder and louder.

'Umby-byumpa — umby-byumpa.'

The indecipherable cry of the rag and bone man resounded along the street. The Steptoe like character in brown corduroy jacket and flat cap, checked the reins of his ambling, flea-bitten, mare, as they made their way up the street.

This man turned up like clockwork, come rain or shine, with a cart full of old scrap metal.

We would never sell our old rags to him. Instead we

—''GOT ANY POLISH MISTER''—

Above: The Betterware Man who gave away small sample tins of polish —
snag was, mi mam had to buy something before he would let us have one. She
wasn't always right pleased.

would take our laden sacks to the 'scrappy under the bridge' at Swinton where each full sack would bring us a shiny tanner. This was twice as much as the miserly three pence from the rag and bony.

Another notable visitor to tread our pavement was the Betterware man. We would see him emerge from his office on Brittain Street over a hundred yards away as my sister and I played 'two balls' against the house wall. His off-cream Macintosh would swish with the spring in his step as he fought to hold onto the mops, brushes and suitcase that he amazingly carried in just two hands.

The game stopped as we bounded towards him.

'Got any polish mister?' we would enquire. Inside that battered suitcase he had hundreds of miniature tins of shoe polish. Each tin would only shine a few shoes but the size fascinated us because we would use the empty tin to 'play shops' afterwards.

'Is your Mum in first?' was his usual reply and we would nod as he followed us down our ginnel.

Before we had any time to warn Mother that the Betterware man was here, he would be behind us launching into his sales routine.

'Can I interest you in our latest products madam.?'
His movements were swift and meticulous, using a degree of dexterity that would have pleased a stage conjuror. His audience, the simple housewife was entranced by the patter that rolled off the edge of his silver tongue.

With another sale closed, the miniature tin was pushed into my hand. The Betterware Man showed a perfect set of gleaming teeth and bid us 'goodday.'

Mother would huff and puff as she threw another bag of yellow dusters to the back of the cupboard angry with herself for succumbing yet again to his sales pitch. But, at her expense, we had our little tin of polish.

'SPIKE'

'Michael what on earth are you doing?'
I was half-way down the street when I heard Mum's voice.
'Sledging' I shouted back holding tightly onto the reins.
'I can see that, stop it at once, you'll strangle Spike'
The fresh fall of winter snow had brought innovations to sledging. As Schofield Street had no hills I discovered that by putting a rope around my dog's neck and making him run, he would drag me to the bottom of the road in no time. I was Scott of the Antarctic with my faithful husky.

We had cared for a number of dogs over various years, at home, but Spike was the dog I can remember most. Being 'Heinz' 57 variety, he was a very loyal and friendly animal. Mealtimes was when man's — or should I say — boy's best friend came into his own. Many varieties of vegetables came from Dad's allotment, but cauliflower, cabbage and sprouts would stay on my plate long after everyone else had finished eating. I hated those greens. I was threatened with all manner of punishments if I did not eat them but each small forkful would stick in my throat, sending an uncomfortable shudder through my body.

There were distractions of course, that would take my mind off the dreaded 'greens' — and one was television. Dad had control of the channels and his selection, whilst we ate tea, determined whether I could forget the nauseous taste in my mouth.

After watching *Robinson Crusoe* for the third time that year — in black and white, I might add, my nervous reaction to the limp vegetables that still swamped my plate could not be hidden for a second and Dad inevitably caught me screwing up my face.

'Get in that kitchen and don't come out until you've eaten those greens' he would scream at me. With plate in hand and closing the door to the kitchen I shut myself in with Spike. The kitchen was his domain and with his help those vegetables would miraculously disappear and I would be in Dad's good books again.

One day however, Spike did the dirty on me. Dad had met me from Garden Street infant school and with Spike in tow we walked back along the old brickyard and onto Blenheim Crescent.

'Can I walk him home' I asked

'Yes but be careful in case he drags.'

I took a hold of the leather leash and began to walk and skip home. Spike halted on a few occasions at lampposts along the way and I tugged sharply to jolt him into a walk. Onto Catherine Street and he stopped again several times, relieving himself on each post. I pulled and yanked but he was far too strong. Wrapping the leash around my hand for a better grip I pulled sharply again and his neck shot forward. Realizing my plight, Dad whistled. Spike instantly bolted towards him. The leash was still around my wrist and it was my turn to suffer whiplash, except, I shot forwards and only stopped when my skinny frame collided with the next lamppost. I received a busted nose, lip, finger and thumb. By the time Mum saw me as she stood on the front doorstep tears were streaming down my face. 'Mam it was Dad's fault' I sobbed, 'my thumb aches, my finger aches,' I said holding up the bloodied and swollen hand 'and my head aches'.

'And you're giving me bloody earache' Dad huffed, 'will you stop whingeing Michael.'

Below: When there was no one else to play with 'Spike' was always around (ar' Glynis didn't count).

GRANDPARENTS

NANAAN and GRANDDAD KING

'Tell us a fairy story Granddad'

'Fairies don't tell stories.' he replied.

'Ah tell us a fairy tale then.'

'Fairies don't have tails.'

It was always the same conversation as the small, bespectacled man eased himself into his chair. I jumped onto his knee and stroked the thick head of snow white hair. I had been told that its colour had changed overnight, while he was in a deep state of shock, having discovered the body of his cousin, who had committed suicide by cutting his own throat from ear to ear.

He pushed his thumb into the bowl of his pipe to deaden the tobacco and laid the briar on the table. Clearing his throat, another story would unfold with such care to detail that I would sit mesmerized until he had finished. He would sometimes retell a ghost story with such frightening clarity that he never failed to make me jump when he shouted 'BOO' at the end.

Albert King and his wife Nellie came to live at 16 Wood Street, Mexborough, from their native east end of London. These two were true cockneys and Granddad would regularly speak rhyming slang, much to my annoyance.

As I sat cross legged and fascinated, the only sound to break my concentration was the steady clickety-clack of knitting needles in Grandma's hands.

Grandma had great difficulty in walking, one leg was shorter than the other and she needed a wheelchair to get about.

I can recall being told that these Grandparents had been bombed out of two houses during the Second World War. Unfortunately my images of war were confined to the pages of the Victor comic and I decided that to be targeted twice must have meant the Nazis were really out to get the Kings.

Above: Nellie and Albert King who travelled north in the 60's to reside at 16 Wood Street. Two Cockneys – Grandad irritated me with his rhyming slang, fascinated me with his fairy tales and terrified me with his ghost stories.

On Sundays, before attending St. George's church, I would call in to see them. They would always ask me to go to a cigarette machine for them. This was a big responsibility. Clutching a full shilling, I ran to the post office, crossed over by the traffic lights and reached the machine which was mounted on a wall next to the hairdressers and the television repair shop on Swinton Road. These shops were a very strange shape because the front was straight but on examination at the rear I discovered that the hairdressers shop had a very thin gable end which then went out at a forty-five degree angle to join up with the other shop. This resulted in one end of the block being very much larger than the other. Having put the shilling in the machine and pulled out the cigarettes, I made my way back stopping at

Above: Spending the 'Kings' shilling.

the post office. At this point on my journey there was a large street plan of Mexborough that had buttons to light up various locations. Finally I would check the two red telephone kiosks and press the B button to see if any pennies would return. I do not think I ever struck lucky.

Unfortunately, my fond memories of Grandma and Grandad King were very few for they both died when I was very young.

I can remember one afternoon returning home from the backings and walking in on hushed voices and solemn faces. We always had visitors at home to see Mum but this particular day there were more than normal. Mum was sitting in Dad's armchair, both hands clutching a cup of tea.

'What's up Mam?' I enquired.

Her eyes had dark lines around them and her face creased as she looked at me.

'Granddad's gone to Jesus darling' she said ever so serious. It was my first experience of being confronted by death and I felt my little world suddenly caving in. As the tears welled into my eyes I stared up to the ceiling to see the book of fairy tales suddenly closing.

NANAAN and GRANDDAD FOWLER

As soon as I neared the rear gate of 2 Wood Street the sweet smell of home-made shortbread wafted towards me from the open kitchen window. The back door was slightly ajar and I peered round it to see Nanaan Fowler slotting another tray of her delicacies into the oven.

'Hello wee 'un did you smell my baking?', she asked in her soft Scottish accent.

My Gran, Isabella Barr-Kerr, or Isa, as she liked to be called, met and married a Yorkshireman, Robert Fowler and initially they lived in her 'neck of the woods.'

They came down from Scotland upon the death of my Great Grandfather to help look after the family business, which was the roller skating rink located on West Road in Mexborough.

They eventually moved into a terraced house next door to David Haighs' furniture warehouse on Wood Street. This house had the unprecedented luxury of a bathroom that was plumbed in.

It was through Granddad that my interest in football began. He was on the committee of Mexborough Town Football Club and an avid follower. He got me a job as a programme seller and ball boy. Every Saturday I watched them play in their blue and gold and I dreamed of one day turning out with them.

I recall the stand being built and can remember that there was even talk of floodlights being erected. The sixties were good for 'the Town' and there was always a big crowd, which was only surpassed by the throngs who visited the

Below: Robert Fowler and Isabella Barr-Kerr Fowler. Grandad Fowler aroused my passion for football and introduced me to fine art.

Above *Back row:* J. Graham, W. Farrier, J. Lindsey, F. Rounds, B. Farrier, S. Roberts, P. Jackson, Hodkin, H. May. *Second row:* C. Caunwood, unknown, Mrs Graham, L. Hague, E. Wilson, C. Pilling, A. Wrath, unknown. *Front row:* E. Smith, W. Wright, R. Fowler, E. Gamble, F. Pilling, H. Caunwood.

ground on Bank Holiday Monday to watch the Montagu Cup.

During the summer evenings in Wood Street I found myself being allowed to join in games of football at the top of the street, where the goals were chalked onto the back of some outhouse walls. Parents even joined in and I would stay until my Father's voice boomed out over the backings. Even though he was a street away his foghorn of a voice would cause my ears to prick up and like a dog with its 'tail between its legs' I would scamper home for my nightly wash in the pot sink.

Below: Rear of Wood Street. The large rooftopped building in the background was the St George's church hall, where I did most of my cub and scouting days. This area and its buildings were demolished in the 1980's and is now a complex of aged persons bungalows.

Above: The family firm of Sinclair pork butchers stood at the junction of High Street and Glasshouse Lane for over a hundred years prior to its demolition in the 1980's. The pies, sausages and other delicacies sold from these premises were all made downstairs in its basement.

Above: The old pawnbrokers shop became David Haighs, retailer of household goods and stood at the junction of Main Street and Belmont Street. David Haighs was a firm with many local shops in nearby towns, however the business folded in the 1980's.

Above: The Albion Inn — 'The Staff' as it was commonly known was situated on High Street and was one of my father's regular 'watering holes'. (It was demolished in the early 1970's to make way for the new shopping complex.)

Above: Swinton Road. The road used to extend to Swinton, however, it is now a dead-end at the approximate location of the bus in this picture.

Below: Swinton Road looking towards High Street. This was once a very busy junction in the town centre because of the bus terminus and had to be controlled by traffic lights. The building in the background is the post-office which still exists, but all the other buildings have long since changed hands. The Midland Bank, (just going right, out of the picture), is now a bookmakers.

THE CLUB TRIP

I awoke to the pitter-patter of the tiny feet of sparrows foraging in the gutter outside my windows. My eyes burst open. A thin beam of sunshine poked through the gap in my bedroom curtains, picking here and there at flecks of disturbed white dust that danced like fairies above me.

SUNDAY — AT LAST.

For several days I had been waiting impatiently for this morning to arrive.

Dressing quickly in new clothes set aside for the occasion I tiptoed downstairs listening to the words of 'Puff the Magic Dragon' drift from the radio, and the hushed voices of Mum and Dad as they moved around the kitchen.

Pushing open the room door, I saw Mother buttering a mountain of bread. The fold-down section of the yellow and white kitchen cabinet creaked in time to the sweep of Mum's butter knife over each slice. Dad was drying the frying pan he had just used for breakfast.

Spike jumped up at me, his warm tongue licking my cheek. I pushed him aside and rubbed at the wet patch he had left behind. Stepping onto the peggy rug I noticed the silver fish scurrying back into the warm crevices beneath broken hearth tiles. Embers from the previous night's fire still gave off a glowing heat as I plonked myself onto the sofa to complete the task of pulling on my socks.

By the time I had finished this, Glynis had arrived downstairs and we both had to sit at the breakfast table. We tore into the toast that had been forced onto us, having been told that we had to eat something. Excited children did not want to eat, I silently screamed at my parents, but they would not understand — they were adults. As we gulped down the last morsels a handful of coins were thrust into our palms. We skipped outside in the direction of the newsagents to look for comics to take on our journey. We were allowed to buy two comics each and being the older brother I encouraged my sister to buy the *Dandy* and *Beano* while I bought the *Wizard* and *Victor*. The *Victor* was a memorable comic. By the time you had turned over the last page you had acquired a smattering of pigeon-german; '*Achtung; Schnell, schnell*' and '*Schweinhund*' were just a few of the words I had mastered.

The short journey to Mexborough railway station was a mixture of running and hopping with Dad repeatedly calling us back as Mum and Dad tried to keep up with us.

Below: Another Club trip and we were both barn't enjoy us sens despite the typical British summer weather.

The station platform was filled with a mass of excited faces, many of which I recognized.

The tannoy crackled into life, but it was hard to decipher the message that came over. However, I realized from the reaction of the crowd that it was announcing the arrival of our train. I felt a sudden tug on my jacket collar as Dad dragged me away from the edge of the platform and then clamped a shovel-like hand on my shoulder to keep me in place.

A large black and grimy engine shunted in, bellowing clouds of thick smelly smoke that left you coughing and choking. We boarded frantically and selected a table by the window.

'Mum he's pinching me' yelled Glynis clutching at her arm.

'Well she's kicking me' I lied convincingly.

'I'll pinch and kick you both if you don't behave' boomed Dad, his voice like thunder and his face reddening. We jumped back in our seats, knowing what would happen if we did not behave. Glynis' tongue darted from between her lips with the speed of an adder and I retaliated with a kick to her ankle and then quickly sat back as the jolting train began chugging away from the station.

A feeling of euphoria came over me as I opened my comic and lost myself in the adventures which unfolded before me.

A short time later the rattle of bottles in wooden pop crates disturbed me as I watched the committee men trundle with their burden along the aisles. Their big bellied frames swung in time with the motion of the train, as they plonked bottles of pop and bags of crisps, that you salted yourself, onto the tables. This was quickly followed by bags of Spanish and lollipops and finally we were handed brown envelopes with our names written on them.

'That's yours' announced Dad 'and once it's gone don't ask me for any more.'

I tore at its seal eagerly and pulled at the contents. Inside was a ten shilling note — a king's ransom. I would never

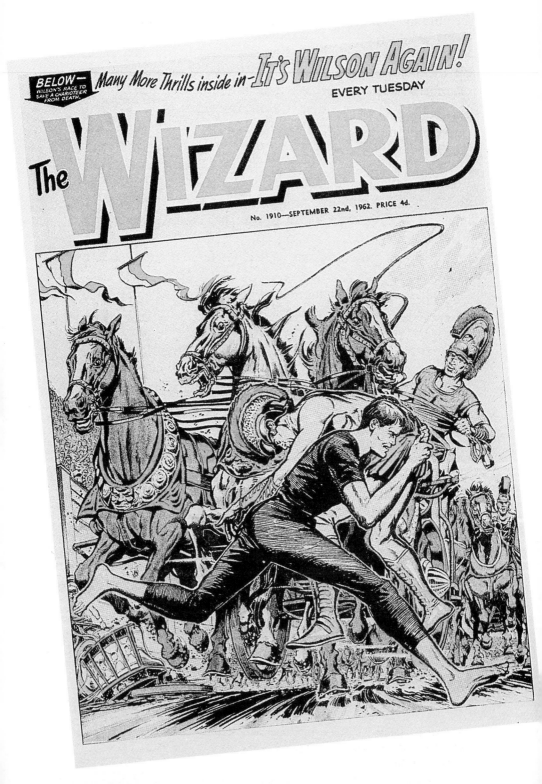

be able to spend this in a whole day, I thought to myself —
but I would try.

The journey seemed endless but we finally arrived at
Cleggy (Cleethorpes for the uninitiated) and headed for the
sands. It's strange but there is something therapeutic in
scrunching bare toes in fine grains of sand and I stood there
surveying the coastline as my feet moved about in the warm
sand.

The 'ten bob' was 'burning a hole' in my pocket and I
pulled it out and waved it in front of Mum's face. Two
shillings and sixpence was immediately spent on a bucket
and spade and a further tanner (sixpence) on some flags to
adorn the castles we were about to build.

Then the construction business began in earnest and
many elaborate sand buildings took shape around us. We
dug large holes to fill with water, but the water always
disappeared. We sat in an assortment of sand boats and
cars dreaming of round the world voyages and grand prix
races.

Then, with lunch time looming, we headed for the public
toilets where we cleaned hands and feet. Replacing socks
and sandals, it was then time for real seaside fish and chips

Above: Ten shillings was a small fortune then and sufficed to give a young lad
a good day out at the seaside. Its equivalent today (50p) would just manage a
small ice cream.

Above: A Club committee man keeps an eye on his charges in his obligatory,
best navy blue suit. If the sun comes out he may even take his shoes and socks off.

— they always tasted better than at home. The day's outing ended with lots of rides at Wonderland. I somehow managed -to spend that ten shillings, but left the sea front with candy floss and a paper plate full of rock bacon and eggs.

This was the one and only occasion I can recall going on the club trip by train. After that we went by one of the buses from the endless row that lined Garden Street where throngs of people spilled over onto the roads and the committee men were kept busy, their arms and mouths working in unison as they attempted to quell the pandemonium and put 'bums on seats' of the coaches.

The journey always seemed longer by bus and on the return trip there was a brief interlude at a public house. The remaining journey was filled with adult tongue-in-cheek songs. I was amazed why they should find some of these so funny.

'What does that mean then Dad?' I enquired.

'You'll find out when you're old enough — aren't you tired?'

'THE CLUB TRIP'

Above: The endless row of buses for the 'club trip' were caught on Garden Street

VISITING THE 'FLICKS'

'...A bet thar would be scared if thar came down here at neet.'

'Bet thee I wunt.' Graham dragged his long woollen sleeve across his running nose and sniffed loudly.

'Thar only saying that because thar knows thar would be.'

'Ghosts dunt scare me.' he screwed the long sleeve into his fist, pulling the already strained threads on his pullover.

'Thar's never seen one.' interrupted Robert.

'Bet thee I have.' he snapped back quite adamantly.

Five of us stood at the red brick entranceway looking into the darkness of the 'monkey tunnel'. Each of us conjuring up our own eerie images of what lay awaiting within the depths of the black hole. The tunnel was built as a short cut for the barge horses who found difficulty in negotiating the sharp bend on the towpath between Mexborough and the Don Pottery works at Swinton. We had stood at this point on many occasions, daring each other to walk the short distance through the unexplored route of the tunnel. All the stories of ghosts and ghouls, had proved effective in deterring us from any investigation.

We turned our attention away from the tunnel and began spinning stones across the murky, oily stillness of the canal.

'Thar's never seen a ghost Graham, thar's making it up' Tony whipped his flat brick across the surface.
For a second Graham was grave and quiet, then his voice exploded,

'I knew thar wunt believe me' and with deliberate aim he sank half a brick with a splash.

Saturday was always the day that I and a group of four friends went to the 'flicks'. This was a flee-pit of a place called the Majestic which was situated on Bank Street, where, for a tanner (six old pennies) we would see cartoons (in colour), a mystery serial that usually lasted for about six weeks, Old Mother Riley, and then a good cowboy or science

Above: The Majestic Cinema was the last picture house at Mexborough and
is now a snooker hall and private club. It was here that we enjoyed our Saturday
matinees: the likes of Mighty Mouse and Old Mother Riley provided the laughs,
Darango Kid and the Man in the Iron Mask the thrills and we supplied the
action with our stink bombs, 'lacky bands' and apple cores.

Above: Market Street. The long building in the background was the indoor market for over a hundred years. When the new market hall was built in the 1970's it became redundant and is now a bingo hall. The joke shop was in the row of buildings that can just be seen to the right of this photograph.

fiction film.

With a spring in our steps we took the short cut through Holmes pop factory along Glasshouse Lane and into the market. Here we browsed amongst the stalls, buying an apple each. These were promptly bitten to the core and pushed into our pocket to provide ammunition for later.

The girl in the black crocheted dress with black underwear beneath, wiggled her slender hips as she walked past us. We looked at each other for a second then elbowed each other before stifling our giggles. I saw several of the male stall holders shoot a glance in her direction, necks almost snapping as they strained to look.

She exaggerated the swing in her short bob of blonde hair as several whistles were blown and I heard the man with a DA cut and a long blue drape-coat say that she looked like 'Twiggy'

'Twiggy' I thought to myself — 'more like a stick' — and I chuckled.

'I'm not surprised every bloke's looking at her, she looks flipping stupid in that holey dress — she must be a crap (a banned word in our house) knitter!'

The rest joined in the laughter.

'Thy face is just like that mask' Graham turned to Rob and pointed to a row of ghoulish masks displayed on a shelf in the joke shop on Market Street.

'And thine'll be like that if tha dunt shut thee gob' retorted Rob, pointing his finger towards a mummy's face, with bandages soaked in blood.

Chuckling loudly we pushed open the door, to a resounding ping as a brass bell on the wooden jamb announced our entrance. The proprietor watched with eagle

Above: Market Street. The original open-air market was in this locality but when the construction work began on the by-pass it was moved to an adopted site at the side and rear of the Montagu Arms. The market's present location is in the pedestrianized High Street.

Below: Market Street. All the houses and buildings at this location were demolished in the 1970's for the by-pass to be built.

eyes as we scoured the cabinets crammed with jokes and pranks.

Pooling our spare cash together we bought two stink bombs and then left, still under the owner's watchful glare. As we made our way along to the cinema we examined our packages, nudging each other as we talked in whispers. We knew we would be releasing the stink bombs during the most exciting parts of the film. Without fail this would bring the manageress flying to the front as the stench of rotten eggs floated to the back of the stalls. Her torch would be imitating a searchlight we had seen in war films and her shrill voice would be shouting for the culprit to come forward. As her dark silhouette obstructed the action on screen, hisses and boos would ring out around the cinema.

Finally we would join the bustling queue near to the cinema's entrance hopefully getting a glimpse of female flesh from the Saturday night special posters. There was the promise of a forthcoming Beatles double-bill and as they were my favourite group I made a mental note of the date.

It was at this point we would reveal our secret weapons — 'lacky bands.' These could easily be hidden round our wrists until it was time to unleash them and then we were ready with specially prepared waxed carton bullets from 'Jubilee' (or 'Jubblies' as we called them) cartons. A well aimed shot brought a tremendous howl of pain from the unsuspecting victim. Hopefully, it was not you.

The remaining three hours were filled with whooping indians, cracking six-shooters and ricochets whining down from the large screen and at times I gripped the seat in front, ducking my head as I came under fire.

At four o'clock, just as I was beginning to suffer battle-fatigue, the lights flickered on and the whistles went up as it was time to head for home, re-enacting the roles our heroes had been playing all afternoon. Then, at home huddled up on the sofa in front of a blazing coal fire, I would await Jimmy Clitheroe, Dr Who and Dixon of Dock Green. There was always such a lot to cram in on Saturdays.

Above: Bank Street. On Saturdays, on the way home from the cinema, I would visit Clays toy department. I can recall buying the original James Bond and Batman car there.

'NESTING'

Early one fine summer's morning, on the corner of Garden Street Infants' School, Kevin appeared to be balanced precariously, almost heron-like, as he rubbed the shoe of his bended leg down the grey wrinkled sock of his upright one. The first knuckle joint of his index finger moved around up his right nostril. Within seconds the finger was out and he gazed at his capture. His eyes suddenly fell upon Paul and myself snaking towards him, his concentration disturbed by the noise of the can we kicked in the gutter. His hand plunged swiftly into the pocket of his short

Below: Garden Street Infants School has now made way for an aged persons complex of bungalows.

trousers, as he wiped his fingers on the lining.

'Aw reight then' he sniffed, a flush appearing on his cheeks.

This was the same Kevin who only a week before had raided his Mother's cupboards and packed a shoe box almost to the brim with icing sugar, instead of the customary flour, to display his prize egg collection. He boasted proudly to class eight as he leaned backwards on two legs of his chair, the shoe box open in front of him.

This was the same Kevin who suddenly crashed to the floor as a swarm of kids enveloped him and a mass of hands dived into the box to sample its sweetness. He watched in horror as the clawing hands split the box sides and a white mushroom cloud reminiscent of Hiroshima exploded towards the ceiling.

Mrs Thompson, our class teacher, flew in with the force of a hurricane, her hands ferociously picking out heads with which to connect and screaming in anger as fine white powder settled all around.

Kevin found himself being pulled up sharply by one ear and was dragged off to the headmaster as his classmates continued to rifle the remainder of the icing sugar. The blown eggs lay shattered and this hurt Kevin more than the punishment that had been meted out.

'What's tha playing at then?' he continued, pulling a clean hand from his shorts.

'We're going nesting. Does tha want to come?' we replied almost in unison. With a nod, he slotted in behind us and with a shuffling of feet he followed in our wake.

'Nesting' was a very popular pastime for young boys in the 1960's and was not unlawful. We would walk miles to collect a variety of birds eggs to add to our collections. This particular journey, with Kevin in tow, took us along Mexborough's Dog Daisy and into Barnburgh Woods, where the early morning call of the cuckoo 'whet our appetite'.

Three pairs of eyes darted in all directions and hands

pulled at bushes as we sought that special nest. Kevin's cry alerted us and we followed the line of his arm and pointing finger to the bundle of twigs and straw neatly sitting between treetop branches

His feet were running across the lower branches even before we had decided who should make the climb and his light frame skilfully flitted between interlocking boughs as he wove his way through the greenery into the uppermost part of the tree.

He was soon only a shadow and his shouting disturbed the sounds of summer within the woods,

'Magpie, it's a three egger.'

That was one each. I looked towards Paul and our eyes lit up.

Kevin was only able to hold one egg in his hand if he was to make the return journey to terra-firma safely. So he placed the other two in his mouth mimicking a retriever carrying game. With cheeks bulging like a hamster he began to negotiate the branches as he clambered downwards, listening to our instructions as he loomed closer. With just one branch to go before the short drop onto the grass he decided to swing down with an outstretched arm. This went disastrously wrong. He slipped, arms and legs flailing and grasping at fresh air as his jaw smashed onto the wooden stump. The eggs in his mouth exploded with a muffled pop. With his jowls filled with a mulch of raw egg and shell he collapsed to the ground vomiting a yellow mush from between his gaping lips. The sight of us doubled up with laughter only increased the volume of the curses he threw at us. It was difficult to hide the tears of laughter that trickled down our cheeks.

TROLLEY MAKING

The sawing and banging noises interrupted the cup final between Mexborough Town F.C. and Leeds United which was being staged in the back yard of 23 Schofield Street. Suddenly the match ground to a halt as the noise increased and I peered curiously over the wall to watch the activities of my neighbours, Michael and Martin. They were quite posh because while we still had to drag up a tin bath on Sunday nights, they had an enamel bath, covered with a board when not in use, fitted into the kitchen.

'What's tha doing?' I enquired.

'We're mecking a trolley' they replied, without looking in my direction.

Without waiting for an invitation, I joined them to watch

Below: The back yard of 23 Schofield Street was the training ground to develop my footballing skills. It was here that the new signing for Mexborough Town (me) began his run at the halfway line, swerved through the defenders and crashed a low volley into the back of Leeds United net. How the crowd roared.

the secrets of trolley making unfold as small pieces of wood slotted together onto old pram wheels. A piece of threadbare carpeting tacked down for seating provided a touch of class. I watched in awe as a red hot poker sizzled a hole into the front section of this vehicle and a bolt was knocked through to allow a rotating movement. Finally a length of rope was fastened at each end close to the wheels to complete the steering mechanism. The *pièce-de-resistance* of this marvel of modern transport was a hand brake. A piece of wood was crudely nailed to the back box section and with a forceful thrust of the hand the wood clamped itself down onto the rubber tyre of the back wheel, inevitably slowing down its speed.

Having watched this, several days later and with no blue prints to hand, I started to tackle a similar project. The hardest task was finding a spare set of pram wheels. A good pram was always kept for unforeseen eventualities — someone on the street was always pregnant.

A good six hours later a friend and I had completed our trolley and so began its test run. The most frustrating part of this was pulling it along several streets and onto the gradual slope of Barbers path that ran above Gorney's rocks. Our run took us down the path, building up immense speed. Our only problem was avoiding the sideswipe of some old dear who happened to be on the path at the time. We would zoom past her leaping figure, heads down to avoid detection. A torrent of abuse faded as we gained distance and shot down onto West Road. The tricky part came with the turn onto Blenheim Crescent as the rear wheel lifted and the trolley crabbed and bounced around the corner. Our knuckles turned white as we grasped the framework for fear of flying off. The route was about a quarter of a mile long and we were fortunate that we were usually untroubled by any motor cars.

I can recall one day that we had decided to try the trolley from the top to the bottom of Oliver Street. This is a particularly steep road and with three of us on the trolley

Above: 'A helping hand' — my very own trolley, the piloting of which would result in me receiving a prestigious wound that would enable me to impress the girls for many weeks to come.

that day it was a very harrowing experience. I was the rear
man and the up-shot was that as we began to roll forward
I decided that I no longer wanted to be part of it. Stupidly,
I attempted to stop the trolley by grabbing hold of the rear
wheel.

Unfortunately my hand became trapped in the spokes and
was dragged onto the road surface. The sharp pebbles ripped
at my flesh quickly dashing any future thoughts of a
sponsorship deal with Stirling Moss. My trolley days were
over.

I must say though, once the pain had disappeared, I was
proud to keep unwrapping the discoloured bandage, in the
playground of Garden Street School, to show off my future
'scar'.

In fact I actually nursed the wound, continually picking at
it to make it bleed. After the six weeks' summer holiday I
still managed to carry the scab to Adwick Road Junior
School.

Opposite Page: This aerial view begins on Glasshouse Lane and takes you up
into High Street, then onto Garden Street and Dolcliffe Road and finally Park
Road. All the houses at the bottom left of this picture were demolished for the
by-pass. Also in this picture the houses on Dolcliffe Road (opposite the
allotments) have also been demolished and new semi-detached homes are in
place. At the top left with the criss-cross paths is the old brickyard and top
centre you can just see 'Gorneys' rocks.　　　　　　　　*Aerofilms*

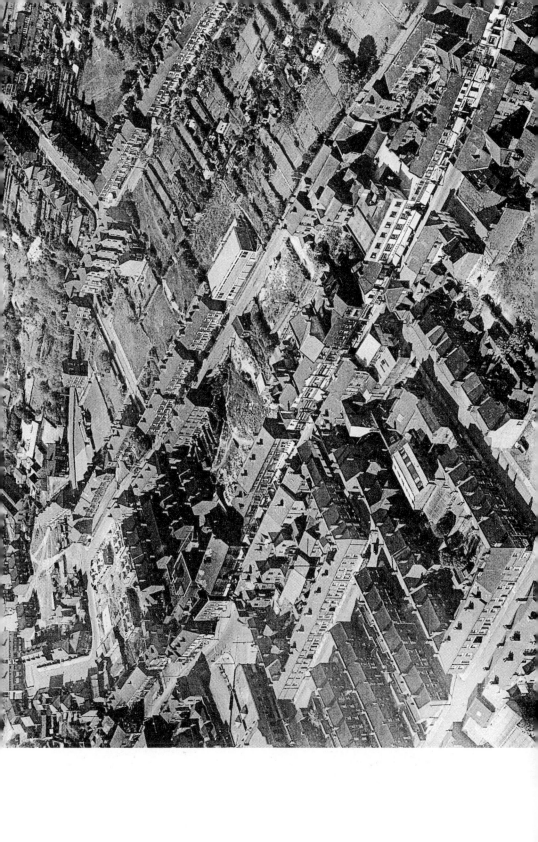

Above: The Montagu Arcade, Bank Street. The top chambers of this arcade were a billiard hall.

Above: Cantors and shops adjoining made way for new buildings and the narrow roads of the High Street have become pedestrianized.

Above: Walker's shop was situated on Main Street and was where my sister and I spent our weekly pocket money of sixpence. The chemist shop to the right has become a dentist, whilst Walker's and a row of houses behind it were demolished and a community centre is in place.

BROWN SHOES

'Michael come here' Mothers voice exploded in my eardrums.

I trapped the bouncing tennis ball underfoot and sauntered towards her. She was standing on the kitchen doorstep with her hands on her hips. As I stopped in front of her she yanked my head to one side and for an instant I felt it would snap from my shoulders.

'You are not going out with me looking like that.'

'What's up Mam?' I enquired, my head still bent at 45 degrees.

'Just look at that tidemark.' I winced as she rubbed the corner of a wet tea towel around the back of my neck.

'You've never washed, have you?'

'I have Mam honest. Aaargh you're hurting me.'

'A cat's lick more like. If you think I'm traipsing up the street with you looking like that you've got another think coming.'

Below: Posing for the camera in Gorneys Rocks Park, which was by Barbara's Path. I wasn't scared... I was just holding back until our Glynis had picked up courage to follow me.

Above: High Street, Mexborough. There is still a bus stop at this location but the route now goes along Garden Street because of pedestrianisation. The National Provincial Bank which can just be seen far right is now the National Westminster.

It was towards the end of the summer holidays and Mum had decided that I needed a new pair of shoes for the forthcoming term.

Having rubbed my neck red raw, she then wrapped her hand around mine and with some reluctance on my part, but unable to escape from her vicelike grip, we began to lay siege to a range of footwear shops that were scattered along Mexborough High Street. Here, beleaguered staff traded with a budget conscious housewife.

I distinctly knew what I wanted as I looked longingly at some smart fashionable shoes with animal prints on the sole and a compass concealed in the heel. Unfortunately Mum had other ideas.

'I can't afford those' she exclaimed and grabbing my arm she trailed me further along the street.

Just as I was getting really fed up and mum really frustrated, she guided me into a dimly lit shoe shop. So dim in fact that you could hardly see what you were trying on. This, I realized later, was obviously a cunning ploy, because I came out with the most grotesque and hideous pair of brown shoes one could imagine.

I was sure a pair of clogs would have looked smarter. How could a young boy of an impressionable age 'be cool' in these, I thought.

As the end of the six week holiday drew near Mum had decided that she would take my sister and me for a walk over the ferry in order to 'break in' our new shoes. We went along Church Street, turning by the Ferryboat public house and crossing the footbridge that spanned the canal and the River Don. I had been into this area many times before to capture tadpoles and frogs, taking them from their marshy homes and forcing them into a small glass prison.

However a further treat was in store, for armed with a bag full of potted meat sandwiches and a bottle of diluted orange, we were going to trample amongst the undergrowth of bluebell woods in Old Denaby, finishing the day with a picnic.

'So long as no one saw me in these shoes' I thought, then a promising and exciting day lay ahead.

The only annoying part was being accompanied by Mum's friend Pat and her tribe of four children who slowed the whole journey down. Eventually the eight of us trekked onto Church Street and over the newly constructed footbridge which spanned the River Don. Only a few years ago, a ferryboat was needed to transport people across. It was here that Glynis and I were finally allowed to leave the sound of the continual squeaking wheel from Pat's pram and head towards the woods.

I would regularly earwig on Mum's conversations over the wall to our neighbour Ena and Pat's name often cropped up in their gossip.

'She's having another babby you know, that's five now.' Mum would mumble her words through a wooden peg held in the corner of her mouth as she hung out her washing.

'When I think of the difficult time I had with my two, she has 'em like shelling peas.'

Above: Mum, (far right) and Ena would frequently gossip about 'important' local issues. I can't ever remember Ena leaning on the wall like Norman Evans used to do in *Over the Garden Wall* (my mam and dad would remember that music hall act).

Ena would nod in agreement.

'I don't know how she can afford it. That idle, good for nothing husband of 'ers won't work. If he went out and earned a decent living then he'd have other things to think about.'

The late morning and lunch time went extremely well and I soon forgot the hated shoes on my feet.

Then as we began to make our way home, a beating of wings attracted my attention. A Coot stirred from nearby reeds. It could only mean one thing, a nest was nearby.

I tiptoed into the reeds where the ground was soggy, but reasonably firm. Suddenly with a loud belch and a strange sucking noise, the ground burst open and within seconds my legs were trapped in dark thick mud. I had an uneasy feeling of being pulled to a watery grave and to say I was frightened was an understatement.

'Mam' I screamed 'I'm sinking.'
She moved at the speed of light and grabbing my outstretched hand, tugged me from the earth's grip with a dull 'plop'.

'You daft bugger' she was yelling.

I looked down at myself and from just below the knee I was covered in a dark brown sticky and filthy substance. Then as I looked further down, I saw — No shoes.

'Mum I've lost my shoes'
I could not believe my luck. But she was furious.

'You've done that deliberately' she chided.

'I haven't Mum — honest.'

I was threatened with being taken home sitting on the back of Pat's pram but after much protest about how humiliated I would feel, I managed to persuade Mum to piggy-back me to our house.

I later realized how fortunate I had been. On our next visit to the shoe shop we discovered that we had bought the last pair of those brown shoes and after lengthy negotiations with the threat of a red ear, I traded my ideal shoes for a pair of black and white sneakers.

'BULLY BEEF AND CHIPS'

'Gis a go on thee bike.'

The voice from behind sent a shiver through my feeble frame. Turning, my worst fears were confirmed.

'Ar said gis a go on thee bike' the square jaw of the 'cock of the class' jutted forward as he spoke.

At this stage, I considered pedalling as fast as my legs would allow me but then realized he would only carry out his retribution tomorrow at school.

'All right, but I need it back in ten minutes, my tea'll be ready', I lied. Dismounting the saddle of my pride and joy as did my 'backy' Tony.

I held the handlebars as this Neanderthal boy climbed onto the black seat.

'Don't wreck it, or I'll tell my Dad.' I said softly.

I was talking to the same boy who was not even deterred by a caning from the headmaster so what chance did I have of scaring him. He pushed himself off and began pedalling slowly away.

'Thar can tell who thar wants' he shouted back, pedalling faster and turning into Catherine Street.

'Ar bet tha won't get it back' Tony said turning to me. The same thought had crossed my mind.

I next saw the bobbing frame of my feared foe churning the gravel with the rear wheel of my bicycle as he swung around the corner of Flowitt Street, two roads away. I was sure I could see a smile on his menacing face as he looked towards me and began pedalling away again. He was taunting me and enjoying every minute.

'Ar telled thee didn't I' announced Tony.

'Dad'll kill me' I replied looking forlornly at the disappearing shape.

The cogs in my brain were in overdrive. There was only one answer to this solution. I looked Tony straight in the face.

'Will thy help me get it back?' I saw his jaw drop.

'He won't be able to fight two of us. We'll call him near us and then jump him.'

He shook his head in disapproval.

'I'd do it for thee.' I raised the pitch of my voice, hoping to prick his conscience.

He stared back, 'All right, but we just get it back and then run okay?'

I nodded in agreement, even Tony realized it would be foolhardy for two of us to challenge the 'cock'.

The 'cock' was the spitting image of 'Bully Beef', from the *Dandy* comic, even down to his haircut. He came speeding around again after completing another circuit of the backstreets. I strode towards him with Tony just behind and I suddenly realized how Gary Cooper must have felt in *High Noon*.

As I got closer, he stopped, posing arrogantly over the handlebars of my pride and joy.

'Now' I shouted, leaping forward with the speed and agility of a panther.

My bike collapsed with a clatter and I fell sideways towards the gutter, falling on top of the startled 'thug'. As I sat on his panting chest I glanced sideways, half expecting Tony to be recovering my bike and coming to my assistance. Instead I saw the fleeing figure of my trusted friend, running towards home.

In that instant as I stared into a pair of steel grey eyes, it was hard to say who was the most suprised. I do not know how I managed to hide the shock and disbelief of my situation. Realizing what fate I could expect, I instinctively grabbed at the large pair of 'lugholes' which peeped through his thick black hair and began to shake his head back and forth, banging it on the 'causey-edge'.

He squealed in anguish for several seconds, Then I heard him mumble

'Ar gie up.'

'What?' I shouted at him, shaking with a mixture of fear

and adrenalin.

'Ar gie up' he repeated louder.

I leaped from his prostrate body, jumped onto my bike and pedalled 'hell for leather' home.

Making my way to school the following morning I jammed my hands into grey shorts hoping to disguise my fear.

The white metal gate to the entrance of the playground was going to be my gateway to hell. I opened it slowly, looking out for the enemy. Sneaking in and making my way to the classroom, I missed him completely until I heard his voice to my left.

'FOWLER' came the call.

The blood drained from my body as I turned.

'Thar was lucky last neet, thar caught me off guard. Thar better not go bragging.'

His scowling features were etched in my memory as he spun round and walked away. My jelly-like legs almost buckled as I entered the cloakroom.

Above: Class 4, Adwick Road Junior School. There I am on the back row, third from the left and grinning like a Chesire cat, with 'Bully Beef' on my left. As you can see there were some pretty girls in our class — guess which four I fancied!

OUR STREETS

Holidays abroad are for the rich — and I bet they never played in backings like ours. A dozen or so of us jumped and darted in all directions, feet stomping on the cobbled stones, to avoid the leather casey that bounced off the Victorian outhouse wall. 'Tiggy' football was typical of the games we played during the long summer school holidays.

No one in the street went away for long holidays, but spirits never dampened. The sun always seemed to shine, giving plenty of time and scope for endless activities, usually beginning before nine in the morning and going on until dusk fell.

Friends came and went as the weeks progressed. Any arguments were few and far between and fist fights were a rarity.

In a fitting tribute to our world cup heroes of 1966, Schofield Street Rovers were formed during a wet afternoon as we sat in the newly erected shed in Tony and Graham's back yard, listening to the patter of rain beating upon the tarpaulin roof. The team consisted of anything between eight and sixteen players depending on who was around. We had discovered that a cheap football shirt in the garish colours of turquoise and white was being sold from the Army Stores at the corner of Main Street and Wood Street and several of us bought one of these to look the part.

A full game could last most of the day with endless substitutions and absences as people left for lunch and then quickly returned still clutching remnants of sandwiches.

'Ouch — that flipping stung.' Rob rubbed at the red mark that appeared at the top of his leg where the leather casey had hit him.

'I couldn't help it.' I replied holding up my arms in a show of innocence.

'Well tha shun't toe end it.'

I held up one of the old brown football boots that my

grandad had given me. They were big old fashioned things with bulbous toes.

"I can't do ought else with these things."

I had longed for a pair of George Best white plastic boots, which I was convinced would improve my dribbling skills overnight, although disappointed with Grandad's boots I did try to show a smile of appreciation when he gave me them. At least I had a pair of football boots to show off to those who hadn't.

As teatime approached the call of 'next one's winner' would pierce the air. That was it, the shout was accepted, and if the opposition scored, a replay was fixed for the next day. We would leave criticising aspects of each other's play and conducting a post-mortem on the game.

For the umpteenth time I kicked my brown leather casey against the gable-end of the row of terraces. That was until Paul's mother, with a head full of curlers beneath a bright yellow headscarf, stretched her willowy frame over the low gate of her yard.

'Will you gie ower kicking that ball against my wall, I'm trying to watch Coronation Street'' she said in a shrill voice.

'Is thy Paul coming out missus?' I asked, now juggling the ball with my black school P.E. pumps.

'No he's having his tea and then staying in.'

'Just let him come out for ten minutes.'

'No — he's having an early night.'

'But its only quart to eight. Go on missus.'

'No I said.'

I began to kick my casey against the gable again.

'And will you pack that in' her voice was raised annoyingly.

'But I'm only playing wall-ball.'

'I can see that, go and annoy someone else.'

'Let your Paul just come out for five minutes then.'

'No that's final. Now go away.'

I chipped the ball higher up the wall.

'I'll only tap it missus — not boot it.'

Above: Shelley Street, looking towards John Street. This street along with Cliffe Street, Hope Street, John Street and Glasshouse Lane were all demolished for the bypass. A car park is now part of this street's location.

'Look, just bugger off will you.'

'You shun't swear missus — you'll get you mouth washed out with soap.'

She unlatched the gate and I scrambled to collect my ball. Then, pointing a finger at me she continued in that high pitched voice 'Don't you be so bloody cheeky, and get off home before I tell your Dad.'

I backed away clutching the casey by its dangling lace. Then in a sudden act of defiance I retorted

'Thar can tell me Aunt Fanny for all I care.' and poking out my tongue to Paul's mother, who's mouth was now forged into a shocked 'oh', I scarpered back down the road to the safety of Schofield Street school, where I continued my ball skills against the wall of the empty grounds.

Each year during these holidays, the local council resurfaced our road with tar and large chippings. This would put a temporary hold to our games of marbles as we watched the massive machines trundle onto the street. Large cauldrons of tar would belch and bubble as we sat on the edge of the kerb, knees tucked under our chins. Mum told my sister and I to take deep breaths,

'It's good for you' she would say 'it cures colds and it does your chest good.'

My Mother knew all manner of medical cures that never ceased to amaze me.

While we sat and waited we would break lollipop sticks and pick at the sticky tar, writing our names on the 'causey-edge'. When it was time to go in with tar on our hands and legs, Mum would have to rub our limbs vigorously with large dollops of margarine until the blackness disappeared. Playing with tar was no fun for my mother.

Owing to constant flooding and bad drainage at the bottom of Brittain Street, a natural pond had formed where we would fish for newts and demonstrate our building skills by quickly creating rafts that would sway uncontrollably amongst the reeds.

One sunny afternoon during the six week school holiday I returned home and sneaked away with our tin bath. Realizing it was watertight and because of its shape I guessed it would float. So, using a flat piece of wood as a paddle I was pushed out towards the centre of the pond until a swirl of water rushing past the sides of the bath. I instantly found myself bobbling around totally unstable. Within seconds the front end was dipping and being unable to scramble clear, I found myself up to my waist in the slimy and oily water. At the same time anger, frustration and panic all swept through me. Searching beneath the surface, I grabbed at the handle of the bath and began pulling and tugging.

With both hands in the water I looked over my shoulder, and saw my two friends who were standing on the bank laughing loudly.

'Watch leeches dunt suck blood out of thee.' one yelled. A cold shudder ran down my spine and the hairs stood up on the back of my neck.

I tugged harder and with a sucking noise the bath shot free from the bottom. Its movement suprised me and I staggered backwards my hands reaching to grab something that was not there. The aluminium coloured bath shot to the surface as quickly as I disappeared beneath it.

I spluttered and splashed in panic as the stagnant water covered me, but this lasted merely seconds as I emerged to a bright blue sky and the summer heat.

Sitting on the bank I pulled my knees towards me and squeezed the brown water from my sopping clothing.

I swore and threatened my two companions as they looked down at me, still bellowing with laughter.

Then with head bowed, I dragged the bath back home. The horrible scraping noise of metal on stone drowned out the squelch from my pumps.

Above: Weekday wash. In time it didn't half get humiliating and I was pleased when we got a bathroom installed before I was sixteen.

STITCHES

Over the years I have been prone to a number of injuries, from the slightest sprain to the most painful breaking of bones.

My first real injury was as a result of dropping my hot water bottle on the steep stairs at home. At the same time as I stepped onto it I also attempted to pick it up. This resulted in me pulling the rubber bottle from underneath me. It sent me bouncing down the remainder of the steps. I finished my tumble at the bottom with a broken collarbone.

The catalogue of injuries continued with bones in both lower legs broken, toes fractured, another collarbone, several sprained ankles and a badly gashed hand as a result of the trolley accident.

All these incidents resulted in Mother helping me up Barbers Path to the casualty department of Montagu hospital.

'You here again Dulcie?'

I looked up at the bespectacled face of Nurse Foggarty, standing before me in a crisp white apron over her green uniform.

'What's the little bugger done this time?'

I had been there so many times that Nurse Foggarty was on first name terms with Mum.

'He's done what?' said the nurse, hands clamping on hips.

'Kicked the foot off his pot.'

What Mum meant was that I had broken the rubber heel support from the base of my pot which had been on several weeks for a broken leg.

'And how has he done that?' She asked glaring at me.

'Playing football' I whispered, sheepishly looking away in embarrassment.

'Speak up young man, I can't hear mice squeak.'

I repeated it a little louder, my cheeks colouring.

'PLAYING FOOTBALL' — The whole corridor heard

the words of disgust.
'WELL WE'LL SOON PUT A STOP TO THAT.'
As I followed Nurse Foggarty down the sloping corridor
to the potting room I felt like a soldier being escorted by
military police to a court martial.

Half an hour later my plaster cast was repaired, and as I
hobbled back on small wooden crutches I heard her say to
Mother.

'That'll put a stop to his games.'
Sure enough with my revamped pot I had been shown the
red card for four whole weeks.

During a heavy fall of snow in the last year of my junior
schooldays I was walking with a friend along Dolcliffe Road,
close to the allotments and we decided to test the depth of
snow in an area of scrub land. Leaping from the edge of
the footpath, I slid into the snow not seeing what lay beneath
the surface. As I pulled myself up I noticed the snow turning
pink around me. I felt faint and looking down at the rip in
my trousers I realized something was drastically wrong.
To make matters worse the trousers were brand new and
it was my fault that they were torn —

'Dad will raise the roof when he finds out', I moaned.
But two very deep wounds over my kneecap, sent me into
a state of sheer panic.

My friend helped me to his house from where Mother
and an ambulance were called.

My mind was in a whirl and things seemed to be happening
very quickly as I was whisked up to the Montagu once again.

Nurse Foggarty was there, standing near to the reception
desk, as I limped in.

'He really has done it this time.' My Mother said.

In one of the wooden and glass rooms of the department
I lay prostrate as Nurse Foggarty and a Doctor examined
the wounds

'It'll need stitching.' I heard the lady doctor whisper.
Those words exploded into my brain

'STITCHES' — oh no,! My greatest fear. I began

blubbering in panic.

'Don't be such a baby' chided Mrs Foggarty 'You'll only feel a scratch'

SHE LIED — That scratch felt like a red hot knitting needle piercing my flesh and I almost screamed the place down.

'I had an eighteen month old baby make less fuss than you' she rebuked

'That baby was probably a mute then' I thought to myself as the pain eventually died away.

Needless to say, eleven stitches later, I vowed that I had learned a lesson in life and it was a very long time before I ventured into the casualty department again.

Below: Mexborough Montagu Hospital at its Cemetery Road entrance.

MISCHIEVOUS NIGHT

The damp grey November fog that crept down our road dragged with it a bitterly cold wind, that sought out bare flesh and quickly chilled you to the bone.

I clenched my fists in the pockets of my duffel coat and stamped my feet on the ground in an effort to keep warm.

Like the fog, the rest of the gang drifted slowly into the playground of Schofield Street school. This was our pre-arranged meeting place where, in whispers we hatched our plots.

November the 4th — one night of the year that worried many old people.

We would bolt home from school and wolf our tea down before leaving by 6 o'clock. That would leave us with about two and a half hours to create devilish mayhem. Although our pranks were annoying they were never malicious and no ones property was ever damaged.

We delved into our pockets to bring out the red bangers and a box full of matches. Then it was off to select our first victim. Our targets were those individuals who had chastised us or chased us away throughout the year or had threatened to puncture our football during the many games in the backings.

We began to tiptoe into silent mode, our eyes squinting and straining as we tried to identify the houses of our victims, through the shroud of fog around us.

Clutching at rope, we pushed our way through the thick grey blanket to the front door of one of the houses. Then with look-outs posted, the task of tying together two doorknobs of adjacent houses was undertaken. The movement was quicker and more silent than that of an expensive watch. With the deed completed, thumbs were raised and the loud knocks to both doors were carried out in unison. The scampering of feet and chuckles of laughter signalled that it had worked perfectly.

Other activities included tying the dustbin to a door handle and then knocking before running. This caused a wonderful mess. As the evening drew on, bangers were placed in cast iron drainpipes. The resulting explosion gave off such a tremendous echo that the occupants were convinced the walls around them were about to cave in.

Finally, the best prank was saved until last. Our victim of this was always the person who had hurled a constant catalogue of abuse at us throughout the year. They were generally the nastiest and grumpiest on the street.

Selecting and picking up the 'dog muck' with the newspaper was the worst part. Then we tiptoed to the front door and placed our bundle on the doorstep. Holding back the urge to laugh was difficult as we lit the paper, knocked on the door and fled. Our faces, peering from a gennel opposite displayed beams of satisfaction as the door was yanked open, the occupant stunned as he met the flaming package on his step. He then did exactly what we wanted him to do — he stamped on it, not just once, but several times until the fire disappeared. It was only as the smoke rose from the charcoal bundle and the smell wafted into his nostrils that he realised what had happened and we would watch his face drain in anger. We stifled our laughter between cupped hands, as we saw he was in his stocking feet and we scarpered back to the safety of the schoolyard.

When it was time for bed I would lie awake and, like a soldier returning from battle, I would enthusiastically recall the evenings events with gusto to my sister who would giggle quietly.

'Are you two talking up there?', Mother's voice echoed up the staircase.

'No' we replied, dishonestly.

'Well get to sleep or I'll tell your Dad.'

I punched my pillow to reshape it and laid my head into the crater I had formed.

'Which bonfire are tha going to tomorrow?' Glynis suddenly asked.

Left: Boys of the Evening Patrol on Mischievous Night, seen here on our way to the home of our first victim.

'Think I'll go to big 'un on't brickyard'

'And what are you gonna do at the weekend?'

'Think I'll go through Mexborough looking for all the short-cuts for our gang, in case we get chased. We'll probably stop at the market stalls and play "tiggy-off-ground". Does tha want to come with us?'.

'No, market boss might catch us'.

'Scaredy cat, thar nowt but a big babby'.

'I'm not' she exclaimed stifling a yawn.

I closed my eyes and began to conjure up images of all the streets I knew in the town. As I mapped out in my mind, all the short-cuts — ginnels — alleyways and backings, sleep overcame me.

CONCLUSION

These then are some of my earliest memories of growing up in a small town in South Yorkshire. Looking back it almost appears as if Mexborough became caught in a time trap for a while. Is it my imagination, or is it true, that other neighbouring towns seemed to be a decade ahead of us? Tin baths were surely a rarity in most working class homes by the mid 60s, yet they were still common-place in the terrace houses of Mexborough at that time — as indeed was the little room across the yard. The Majestic Cinema still operated as a picture house bringing 'silver screen' entertainment into the community when other cinemas, in comparable towns, had lost audiences to television and resorted to bingo. And which South Yorkshire town (or anywhere else for that matter) could admit to still operating a passenger river ferry in the 60s? Were we among the last to use the trolley bus with overhead power cables?

I hope that you enjoyed, and continue to enjoy, the photographs and paintings which accompanied the episodes in the life of a typical youngster growing up in a South Yorkshire town thirty years ago.

Above: Doncaster Road.

Below: This photograph shows the bus that was used during the parade of the last days of the trolley buses in the Mexborough area (27-3-1961). These terraced houses were opposite the Miners Arms and have since been demolished to make way for several flats.

Above: Bank Street towards Adwick Road and Doncaster Road. This now forms part of the by-pass the garage to the right of this photograph and also shown in the picture below has been demolished. A roundabout is also now at these junctions.

Below: Adwick Road, junction with Doncaster Road.

Above: Doncaster Road.

Below: Doncaster Road. The power station has now been demolished. The gates on the right hand side were one of the entrances to Denaby Main Colliery. This road used to travel over Grays Bridge. This has now been demolished and a new shorter and wider road bend is in situ.

Above: Denaby Main Crossing. The buildings and winding gear to the left hand side was Denaby Main Colliery. The man operated gates have since been replaced by automatic gates. The row of terraced houses in the centre of this photograph has also been demolished.

Above: Market Street.

Below: Mexborough Council Depot on Market Street was demolished for the by-pass and fly-over.

Above: Prospect House, Market Street.

Below: Mexborough Police Station, Market Street. This fine Victorian building also disappeared for the by-pass and re-located, initially in Mexborough Council pre-fabs on Adwick Road, until the new building emerged in the early 1980's.

Above: Mexborough Fire Station, Market Street, also disappeared because of the by-pass and was initially located in portacabins on Adwick Road until its present building on Highwoods Road.

Above Market Street and **Below:** Pinfold Lane. Both these streets disappeared with the bypass.

Above: The canal towards Mexborough Power Station. The chimneys and cooling towers of the station were evident in Mexborough's skyline until its demolition in the 1980's. The land left behind still remains unused.

Above: Mexborough Lock looking towards the Toll Bar. A new lock is located at this position now.

Above: Mexborough Low Lock. The lock-keepers house has since been demolished and the lock has been reconstructed.

Above: The ferry crossing from Mexborough to Old Denaby. This photograph was taken in August 1963 and just shows part of the bridge that was under construction and that is now used instead of the ferry.

ACKNOWLEDGEMENTS

A special thanks to the Mexborough Heritage Society; Geoff Wharnes of Hexthorpe, Doncaster; Duncan Mangham of 'In-Camera'; to Ken Hannet's computer skills for making a hard task easy; and finally to Liz whose encouragement made all this possible.

Wharncliffe Publishing Ltd

47 Church Street, Barnsley, South Yorkshire S70 2AS
Telephone: 01226 734222 Fax: 01226 734438

ASPECTS OF BARNSLEY
Discovering Local History
Edited by Brian Elliott

A selection of articles from twelve local authors on some of the historical aspects of the Barnsley district.
Barnsley Boys Club ✻ Bleachworks Archaeology
Papermills ✻ Turnpike Era ✻ Rylands Glass
Watter Joe ✻ Old Kingstone ✻ A Worsbrough House
Hunshelf ✻ Thorncliffe Riots of 1870
Ebenezer Elliott ✻ Gunthwaite ✻ Dodworth

ISBN: 1-871647-19-3 256 pages 108 illustrations
£9.95 Paperback

ASPECTS OF BARNSLEY 2
Discovering Local History
Edited by Brian Elliott

Sixteen local history accounts covering a wide variety of topics from 17th Century misdemeanours to 20th Century childhood memories.
Public Hall Disaster of 1908 ✻ Barnsley Races
Leisure Activities at Oakwell 19th Century
Early Motoring in Barnsley
Welsh Community in Carlton and Smithies
Quackery, Fiddling and Bloodsucking
Mapplewell and Staincross – 19th Century
Darley Cliffe Hall ✻ Law and Order, Stainborough
Newspaper Publishing in the 19th Century
Beginnings of Banking in Barnsley
Mining Verses ✻ Thurgoland Wire Mills
Silkstone Railway ✻ Agnes Road School in the 1940s
Childhood in Stairfoot

ISBN: 1-871647-24-X 288 pages
146 illustrations £9.95 Paperback

ASPECTS OF BARNSLEY 3
Discovering Local History
Edited by Brian Elliott

More local historical aspects of the district from Elsecar to Penistone which include the following features:
The Dearne-Dove Canal ✻ Pawnbroking
Taylor Row and the Handloom Weavers of Barnsley
Town End in the 1870s
Cures and Curiosities of Old Barnsley
Memories of a Barnsley Childhood
E G Bayford of Barnsley: Memoir and Tribute
Barnsley in the Rock 'n' Roll era
Tankersley Iron Stone Mining
Teaching Local History in Barnsley Schools
Water Powered Sites of the Dearne
The Newcomen-Type Engine at Elsecar
Pigotts-an Entrepreneurial Estate at Dodworth
Penistone Market Place
The Joseph Mitchell Memorial Hall: A Sad Tale

ISBN: 1-871647-26-6 288 pages approx
Illustrated £9.95 Paperback

ASPECTS OF ROTHERHAM
Discovering Local History
Edited by Melvyn Jones

A selection of articles from fifteen local authors on some of the historical aspects of Rotherham district.
Thomas Rotherham College, 1482-1550
Travellers to Rotherham
Water-powered Mills in Maltby
A 17th Century Kimberworth Farmhouse
Sandbeck Hall and Park
The Third Earl of Effingham
The First Marquis of Rockingham's Rent Roll
Kiveton Salvin Hall ✻ Carolling at Thorpe Hesley
19th Century Population Growth at Parkgate
Colliery Waggonways in the Rotherham Area
George Wilton Chambers of Rotherham
A Bomb Outrage at Thorpe Hesley in 1861
History of Coal Mining in the Dearne Valley
Templeborough Steel Works
From Slums to Council Houses
'Roger Dataller', a Local Literary Figure

ISBN: 1-871647-27-4 288 pages approx
Illustrated £9.95 Paperback

RAILS THROUGH BARNSLEY
Alan Whitehouse

The pictoral history of Barnsley's important railway network in pictures, from the earliest days, beginning 1840 at Cudworth, to its demise in recent times.

ISBN: 0-9507892-5-9 158 pages
Illustrated £7.50 Paperback

BARNSLEY'S HISTORY FROM THE AIR — 1926/1939
Brian Elliott

Fourteen rare aerial photographs taken in the 1920s and '30s form the basis for this photographic history of our town between the wars. One hundred and seventy illustrations with supporting text remind us of an age when, cinema played a leading part in our entertainment, pawnbroker shops seemed necessary for survival, and certain local businesses and companies appeared as if they would endure forever. Featured are firms such as Yorkshire Paper Mill, fellmongers at Old Mill Lane, Ryland's Glass and Beatson Clark. Building of the Town Hall and Yorkshire Traction bus station are covered along with the Girls High School and Locke Park. The author has interviewed many local people to add human interest through their recollections of life in Barnsley in the inter-war years. *This will evoke memories for most of us and inform the young of a Barnsley past and gone.*

Large format book ISBN: 1-871647-18-5
96 pages 170 illustrations £9.95 Paperback

COUNTING THE COST
Jackie Keating

The moving account of a local family's fight to survive the miners' strike of 1984/85. Jackie Keating lived through those dreadful days, and even today still lives with the consequences. *Counting the Cost* is her story — a simple, evocative and often moving narrative of life in a stricken community.
Still as moving as when it was written, but now even more emotive in the light of the end of the coal industry in South Yorkshire.

ISBN: 1-871647-15-0 128 pages Illustrated Paperback
NOW £1.95

THE ASCENT OF SAM
A cartoon history of Barnsley man, from his dim past to the defeat of the Spanish Armada
Roni Wilkinson

An alternative history which explains many of Barnsley man's habits and customs, from his observance of laik days and his disinclination to decorate, to his Sunday dinnertime supping and his religious afternoon nap. Why are there no Roman ruins around Barnsley? How far up the Dearne did the Vikings really penetrate? Who is the god of the local people? See the myth of Robin Hood exploded! What was Barnsley man's part in the Age of Discovery? And who really defeated the Spanish Armada! All this in 118 cartoon strips.

ISBN: 0-9507892-8-3 Over 500 frames Paperback
NOW £1.00

PITS 1
New Edition
John Threlkeld

To mark the end of the Barnsley Coal Field we have re-published a new and enlarged edition of *Pits 1*. A final chapter covering the 'People's Revolt' against the 1992 pit closure programme has been included, along with upwards of a hundred extra photographs depicting life among local mining communities. Chapters have been enlarged and new material included.

ISBN: 1-871647-23-1 168 pages
247 illustrations £10.95 Paperback

THE MAKING OF BARNSLEY
Brian Elliott

The third reprint of the ever popular book giving an insight into life in Barnsley prior to the Industrial Revolution. Subjects covered include: medical care; early development of iron, coal, glass, tanning; the craft of cordwainer, the making of clocks, ropes, soap and candles; persecution of Quakers and witches, prosecution of grave robbers; some interesting local characters; trading in the market places and notable inns and innkeepers.

ISBN: 0-9507892-6-7 384 pages
Illustrated £9.95 Paperback

BARNSLEY BOUNDARY WALK

A collection of nine walks around the Barnsley Boundary ranging from 4½ to 14½ miles, taking in some of the area's most attractive countryside and places of interest.

ISBN: 1-871647-17-7 48 pages
Illustrated £3.95 Paperback

DARK PEAK AIRCRAFT WRECKS 1
Ron Collier and Roni Wilkinson

Spanning the years from 1937 to 1963 more than fifty aircraft, both civil and military, came to grief on the nearby moors. Aircraft types from biplanes to modern jet fighters have left their twisted remains in the Peak District National Park. How they came to grief, who died and who survived, how they were discovered and rescued is told in this remarkable book. It, along with its companion, is an invaluable guide for walkers and ramblers, as well as for all those interested in flying and the history of aviation.

ISBN: 0-85052-457-1 160 pages
Illustrated £8.95 Paperback

DARK PEAK AIRCRAFT WRECKS 2
Ron Collier and Roni Wilkinson

The updated and expanded companion volume to *Dark Peak Aircraft Wrecks I*. Further stories of aircraft crashes in the Dark Peak area of the Pennines. Each pile of rusting metal represents a chapter in wartime aviation history: Oxford, Hampden, Wellington and Stirling from Training Command; a Halifax from Bomber Command; Spitfire and Defiant from Fighter Command; a Thunderbolt and Mustang from the USAAF; a USN Liberator, and many more. Map references are given for walkers and aviation enthusiasts.

ISBN: 0-85052-336-2 192 pages
Illustrated £9.95 Paperback